W9-BTF-843

HOW COULD WE HARNESS A
HURRICANE?

By Vicki Cobb
Illustrated by Theo Cobb

SEA
GRASS

CONTENTS

Hurricane Danny over the Atlantic Ocean photographed from the International Space Station. (NASA)

EVACUATION ROUTE

We might as well have a bulls-eye on our home, because it's headed right for us. The National Hurricane Center has been broadcasting updated bulletins on television every 30 minutes. They have given the storm a name, as if it were a person, so that it can be remembered.

We were on hurricane watch for 48 hours, which changed to a hurricane warning at 36 hours. The idea is to give us enough time to get ready. Now landfall is 10 hours away. We are told that the winds are at least 75 mph (121 km/h) and flooding is expected from the **storm surge**—water that winds have pushed ahead of the hurricane, creating a huge wave that could be 10 feet (ft) (3.05 meters [m]) higher than normal.

Have we prepared? You bet!

People near the ocean have been evacuated to higher ground. They wrapped their precious family photos in plastic and put them in the attic before they left. They frantically looked for shelters where they could take their pets.

The windows are covered with shutters or plywood. The patio furniture is inside. We trimmed our trees and bushes of branches that could come loose in high winds and driving rain. Everything that could become a missile has been secured.

We expect a power failure. We have stocked up on flashlights, batteries, and drinking water and filled the bathtub with water to use for flushing the toilet in case the pumps stop working. Containers of water are in the freezer to become blocks of ice that will keep food cold as long as possible. We have identified the closet in our home that is farthest from any window as the safest place to hide from the dangerous winds.

Now we wait...
This is the hard part.
Will we lose power?
When and for how long?
Will a tree crash into our home?
What damage will we have to
clean up or repair?
How much will this cost?

For people who have lived through a serious hurricane, there is the familiar feeling of dread. Did we make a mistake by not evacuating? Some hurricanes, like Katrina, are famous because they cause so much death and destruction.

We won't know about this one until it is over.

WHAT IS A HURRICANE?

This image of hurricane Igor was taken on September 14, 2010 by a crew member of Expedition 24 of the International Space Station.

Eyewall of dense clouds

Eye of the hurricane

Spiral rain bands

Note counterclockwise spin of entire storm.

A hurricane is a huge windstorm, the largest kind on the planet.

The winds move upward in a spiral, like a circular ramp, forming an eye at the center of the storm. The entire storm rotates around the eye. It also has rain, but the amount of rain is not what defines a storm as a hurricane. It is the eye, which is clearly seen in satellite photos, that defines a hurricane.

 Q: *How do these three essential things for life become something that can kill us and destroy property?*

Scientists who study weather understand that there is no quick or easy answer to this question. A hurricane is a complicated system. We can't start understanding hurricanes unless we first look at its parts separately. That's what meteorologists do in a lab, and that's what we're going to do in this book. We'll do some simple activities so you can understand how scientists know about air, water, and energy. Science has developed an understanding of the ways these three pieces work together in a hurricane.

> **All hurricanes are made of just three things that we can't live without: air, water, and energy.**

Engineers use the knowledge we get from science to design solutions to problems—and a hurricane is a BIG problem. So far, they have designed buildings that can better withstand the destructive power of hurricane-force winds. No one has yet designed ways to weaken a hurricane or steer it to someplace where it can die a natural death without harming people or property. But this doesn't mean that people haven't been thinking about it and imagining what could work.

This book tells the story.

AIR AND PRESSURE

Air is a gas that you can't see, taste, or smell. You can only feel it or hear it when it moves.

 Q: *What can you do to air to learn what it is like? How about catching it and putting it in a container?*

In fact, air fills every space in an open container that is not occupied by some other kind of matter. And once you've caught it, you can try and squeeze it to make it fit into a smaller space. Surprise! It pushes back at you.

This push is called **air pressure.** When you squeeze a fixed amount of air into a smaller space, the pressure of the air increases on the walls of the container.

Air can push back at you because air is a form of matter. It has weight, which means that it is attracted by gravity. The earth is coated with a layer of air—the atmosphere—held next to the surface by gravity. Air pressure is the weight of a column of air 1 square inch (sq in.) or 1 square centimeter (sq cm) that goes up to the end of the atmosphere.

At sea level, air pressure is 14.7 pounds per square inch (lb/sq in.) or 1 kilogram per square centimeter (1 kg/sq cm). The atmosphere is divided into zones. The zone closest to the earth's surface is 4–12 miles (6.4–19 kilometers [km])

thick and is called the troposphere. We live at the bottom of the troposphere. It is where weather happens.

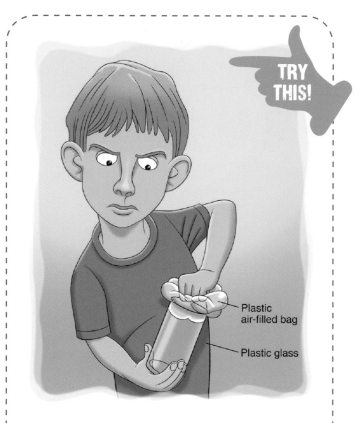

TRY THIS!

Plastic air-filled bag

Plastic glass

Fill a zip lock plastic bag with air. Zip it closed and roll the top over a few times so that the air can't escape. Try and stuff the inflated bag into a smaller container. Feel the air in the bag push back at you.

Toricelli, dressed for cold weather in the mountains, reads his barometer in 1643. Air pressure is lower at high altitudes than it is at sea level. Oil painting by Ernest Board (photo Wikimedia).

 Q: *How did a scientist figure out that air weighs something?*

In the 17th century, an Italian physicist, Evangelista Torricelli (1608–1647), made a glass tube about 32 inches (0.8 meters) long and sealed one end. He filled the tube to the brim with mercury, a liquid metal, which is 13 times as heavy as water. He turned the open end upside down into a bowl of mercury making sure no air escaped into the tube. To his amazement, the mercury in the tube dropped so that it was about 30 inches (76 cm) high, leaving 2 inches (5 cm) of empty space above the mercury. Torricelli correctly figured that this space contained **nothing.**

It was the first vacuum ever created! The column of mercury was supported by the weight of the air pressing down on the surface of mercury in the bowl. (The vacuum produced zero pressure on the mercury in the tube; air pressure was on the glass but not the mercury.) Torricelli had invented the first *barometer*—the instrument that measures air pressure. Today there are many different kinds of barometers.

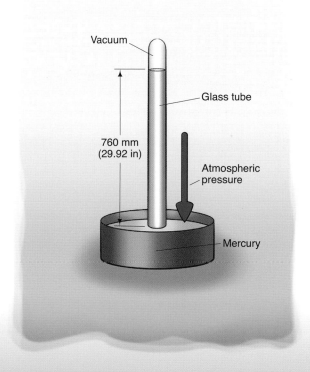

Vacuum

Glass tube

760 mm (29.92 in)

Atmospheric pressure

Mercury

Thermosphere
50 to 440 miles (80 to 700 km

Moon

Mesosphere
31 to 50 miles (50 to 80 km)

Stratosphere
7 to 31 miles (12 to 50 km)

Troposphere
Troposphere 0-7 miles (12 km)

Earth

The Earth's Atmosphere

The atmosphere is a sea of air. We live at the bottom. Air pressure at sea level is higher than air pressure on a mountaintop. That's because the air at the bottom of the troposphere is being squeezed by the weight of the air above it. Air at higher altitudes doesn't have as much air above it to weigh it down, so it is much thinner. You can feel changes in air pressure in your ears when you ride an elevator in a skyscraper, or go up or down in an airplane, or even drive down a mountain quickly. That's why your ears pop—to equalize the changing pressure.

What is the structure of air that explains this behavior?

Scientists imagine that all matter is made of tiny particles that are far too small to see. The smallest particles of air are called molecules. About 78% of air is nitrogen molecules—two atoms of nitrogen linked together. Another 21% of air is oxygen molecules—two atoms of oxygen linked together. The final 1% is made up of other gases, some of which is water vapor. But we'll get to that in a moment. Air molecules are far apart from each other compared to the size of the molecules. Every once in a while, they might bump into each other and bounce away. But it is the huge amount of space between molecules that allows air to be squeezed. The layer above the troposphere is the stratosphere. The air here is extremely thin. Flying is smooth in the stratosphere because it is above the weather.

The sky is blue because air molecules scatter the blue light in sunlight more than any other color. So we see more of the blue. As altitude increases and air gets thinner, the blue gets deeper and deeper, because the black of space is behind the blue. When you leave the earth's atmosphere for space, there is no air and the sky is black. Sunsets on earth are red because when the sun gets low in the sky, light has to travel a longer distance through the atmosphere. Since most of the blue light is already scattered, the reds and oranges of the sunset are the colors that are left.

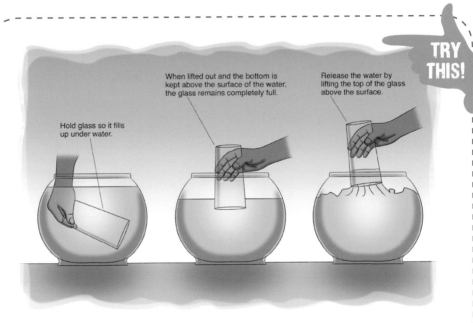

Hold glass so it fills up under water.

When lifted out and the bottom is kept above the surface of the water, the glass remains completely full.

Release the water by lifting the top of the glass above the surface.

TRY THIS!

Try Torricelli's experiment with a glass of water. Hold a glass under water so it fills up. Turn it upside down and lift it out of the water, bottom up, keeping the brim under the water's surface. You will create a column of water above the surface that is the height of the glass. There will be no vacuum on top. You would need a tube about 34 ft (10 m) high to use water as a barometer. Lift the glass above the surface of the water and the seal is broken and the water falls out.

WATER CHANGES TO A GAS

After air, the second component of a hurricane is water. Most of the water on earth is a liquid that covers a little more than two thirds of the earth's surface. Unlike water vapor, where the molecules are far apart from each other, liquid water molecules are in direct contact but can slide past each other. At the surface, where water meets the air, molecules break free of the liquid and enter the air as water vapor. This process is called **evaporation.**

 Q: *What can you do to speed up evaporation?*

TRY THIS!

Wet your finger. Hold it still. How does it feel? Wave it in the air. Does it feel even cooler? Wet your finger again. Blow it dry with a warm hair dryer. Hand blow-dryers in rest rooms are there to speed up evaporation.

It takes energy for a water molecule to break free of the liquid and move into the air as a gas. One form of energy is heat. Your finger feels cool when it is wet because the water molecules are using the heat from your finger to fly off into the air.

Another form of energy is motion. When moving air (wind) strikes the surface of water, some of the fast-moving air molecules collide with water molecules. The collision transfers some of the energy of the moving air molecules to the water molecules so they have enough speed to become free of the surface. It's like setting a resting ball in motion by hitting it with a moving ball. After the collision, a water molecule that is now a gas keeps the energy that was used to free it from the surface as it whizzes about. Also, wind blowing across a body of water lowers the air pressure on the water, so more water molecules evaporate.

Water vapor has much more energy than liquid water.

This is a very important idea to help us understand hurricanes. The amount of water vapor in the air is called **humidity.** Warm air can contain a lot more moisture than cold air. Warm moist air is less dense and has lower air pressure than cooler air.

When meteorologists find a mass of warm, moist air, they call it a *low*. When a low-pressure area moves into your neighborhood, the barometer drops; rain is likely.

You've seen condensation on an ice-cold drink glass during the summer. Water vapor molecules that come in contact with the cold glass give up their heat as the water becomes a liquid on the surface of the glass. Dew is another form of condensation, as is rain.

Water vapor molecules can become a liquid again in a process called **condensation** (the opposite of evaporation). The energy that was put into the water molecule to turn it into a vapor is now released as heat.

One Way Wind Speeds Up Evaporation

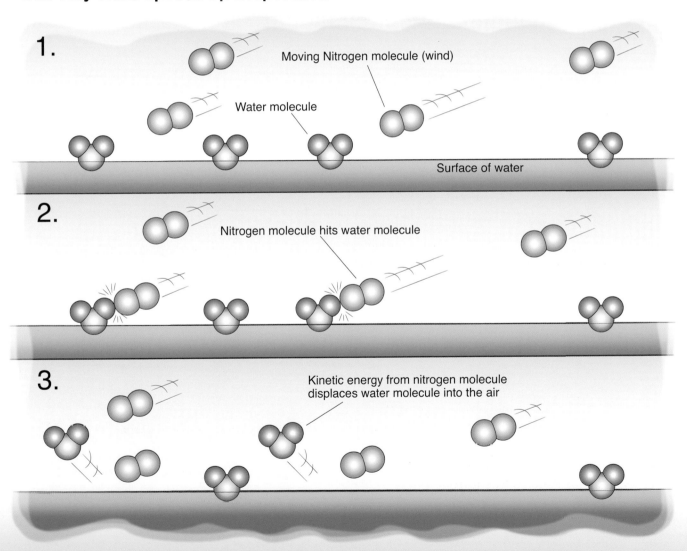

1.
Moving Nitrogen molecule (wind)
Water molecule
Surface of water

2.
Nitrogen molecule hits water molecule

3.
Kinetic energy from nitrogen molecule displaces water molecule into the air

ENERGY AND WIND

Energy is the third major component of a hurricane. One of the greatest discoveries of science is that energy can take many forms—heat, motion, electricity, light, sound, and nuclear energy, to name most of them—and that **one form of energy can be changed into another form without any energy being lost.** A toaster, for example, changes electrical energy into heat energy. Engineers know exactly how much electricity is needed to produce a certain amount of heat. Heat energy is measured by temperature. Scientists have units of measurement for each type of energy. Using math, they have figured out exactly how much of one kind of energy equals each of the other kinds—a major achievement! Math is the language of science.

So, what about heat in the atmosphere?

 Is the atmosphere the same temperature from bottom to top? No!

Air temperature gets colder as you get closer to the top of the troposphere. So if the average temperature is 59°F (15°C) at sea level, it is –70°F (–56.6°C) 12 miles (19 km) up—a big difference! This is even more pronounced at the equator, where the temperature at the top of the troposphere can be more than –100°F (–73.3°C) —one of the coldest places on the planet!

Warm air at sea level is thinner or less dense than colder air. This is because warmer molecules are farther apart and air pressure is lower. As a result, warm air rises.

Water under a mass of low-pressure air evaporates more quickly, and the warm moist air rises, causing an upward motion called *convection current.*

Surrounding air rushes in to follow the rising air. When the rising air comes in contact with colder air higher up, the moisture in the air condenses into droplets of water, which we see as clouds. In clouds, water droplets come together to make larger droplets, and when they are heavy enough, they fall to earth as rain.

Whenever a mass of air moves from one place to another, air from the surrounding area rushes in to fill up the empty space. So wind forms at the bottom of the convection current as air moves to replace the space emptied by the rising air. Water vapor in the air acts exactly like other gas molecules. It expands and rises, and surrounding air rushes in to take its place. During all this motion, the transfer of heat energy is going on all the time.

Locally changing conditions are known as weather.

Weather is the earth's way of distributing heat from warmer areas to colder ones.

Here is an easy way to see convection currents, only instead of using air, we'll use water:

TRY THIS!

You will need:
- Small plastic container (for example, an empty 2-in. plastic pill container with a snap-on top)
- Hammer and nail to punch a hole in the snap-on top and a knife to enlarge the hole so it's about half an inch wide.
- A large clear glass container
- Food coloring
- Several screws to weigh down the plastic container.

Procedure:

Fill the large clear glass container with cold water.

Put the screws and a few drops of food coloring in the small plastic container. Fill it to the brim with hot water and snap on the top.

Holding the plastic container upright, lower it to sit at the bottom of the container of cold water.

Watch as the hot colored water rises in a stream of a convection current.

Put a few ice cubes at on the water and see how it affects the moving current of colored water. After a while, you will see that the color gets distributed evenly throughout the water.

See the effect of temperature on the volume of a gas.

Blow up a balloon.

Measure it with a string or tape around its fattest part.

Write down your measurement.

Put the balloon in the freezer for an hour. Measure it again.

Did it shrink?

Let it sit at room temperature for a while. Does it return to its original size?

Atmospheric air is not in a container, like a balloon. It moves from one place to another to even out air pressure. Moving air, by definition, is wind.

Weather, which takes place in the troposphere, is caused by the uneven heating of masses of air. Air moves to low-pressure areas from higher-pressure areas, causing wind. Weather is the earth's way of distributing heat from warmer areas to colder ones.

At different levels of the troposphere and stratosphere, there are strong winds that move masses of air around. Some of these winds are so steady that they have names—like the trade winds that blow west from Africa or the jet stream that blows east across the United States. These winds also play a part in local weather. A hurricane forms from local air masses that come together.

THE BIRTH OF A HURRICANE

Florida

Bahamas

Cuba

200 km

A few hours later the eye of Irene has clearly developed and it is now an official hurricane.

The summer sun beats down on the Sahara Desert sand, causing hot air to rise above it in shimmering waves. South of the Sahara there is a wide strip of rain forest. Warm moist air rises in steamy mists. Both masses of air travel west to the Atlantic Ocean, pushed by the trade winds. The hot dry air mass instantly absorbs water vapor from the ocean surface, producing fast-rising convection currents.

Tropical storm Irene is a swirling mass of clouds on August 22, 2011 but no eye has developed. (NASA)

The cooler mass of warm moist air from the rain forest moves in to take its place. The combined motion of one air mass moving up and the other moving in above the rotating earth puts a spin on the air. **The earth is spinning faster at the equator than it spins at the poles.** The difference in speed of rotation at different latitudes creates a force on fluids (both water and air) called the **Coriolis effect.**

In the **northern hemisphere**, the Coriolis effect causes tropical disturbances to make a turn to the right, causing hurricanes to spin in a **counterclockwise** direction.

In the **southern hemisphere**, hurricanes spin in a **clockwise** direction and are called *typhoons*. In the earliest stage of a storm, the only thing meteorologists notice on their radar screens is an area just off the west coast of Africa with very low air pressure and very warm temperatures with rising humidity. They call it a *tropical disturbance*. It's something they keep their eye on.

When a tropical disturbance first starts to spin, it becomes more organized in its structure and is now called a tropical storm. If it is to develop into a hurricane, it becomes even more organized. Rising air in the center causes wind to rush inward in spiral bands. The faster the air rises in the center, the stronger the incoming winds, creating a tight spiral around a calm low-pressure area that is the eye of the hurricane. When meteorologists spot an eye in the center of what was once a tropical disturbance, they know they have a hurricane. Clouds form as the spiral of rising moist air draws in the colder air at higher altitudes.

> The clouds nearest the eye form the eye wall and contain the strongest winds.

This is a TRMM (Tropical Rainfall Measuring Mission), which is a satellite image of Hurricane Katrina. It shows the cloud structure that is colored to show how much rain is falling. The huge amount of rainfall in the red hot towers is due to the huge amount of condensation that occurs when warm moist clouds come in contact with the very cold air in the upper atmosphere. Hot towers don't have a long life—anywhere from half an hour to two hours. This TRMM satellite image shows two hot towers of Huricane Katrina on September 15, 2005. The tower on the left is in the eye wall. Hot towers produce enormous quantities of rain as they collapse and condense.

Violent updrafts in the eye wall carry warm moist air higher and higher. When the clouds reach the frigid temperatures at top of the troposphere, massive condensation occurs. The heat energy stored in the water vapor from the ocean's surface, carried up by the convection current, is now released. Heat at top of hurricane causes a rapid expansion of air coming up from below that sucks up more warm moist air up from the ocean. The tops of these clouds are called **hot towers.** They act like high-speed elevators drawing even more hot air up from the ocean surface. (Sometimes a spreading cloud in the shape of an anvil forms at the top.) So a hurricane is a heat engine, transporting heat from the

> The amount of energy released by one single hurricane is no small matter. It can be the equivalent of all the electrical energy used by the entire world in a year!

ocean to the stratosphere and turning much of the heat into wind.

The trade winds push the storm west across the Atlantic.

This TRMM is the same as the one on the left only the clouds have been removed. You can see the Louisiana coastline.

Q: **What makes a tropical storm become a hurricane?** There are four conditions that MUST be present for an eye to develop and the winds become strong enough for a storm to be called a hurricane:

1. The ocean surface water temperature must be at least 80°F (26.7°C).
2. The air around the hurricane must be reasonably moist. If it's too dry, it will get drawn into thunderstorms that create strong downdrafts that kill the convection. Thunderstorms over the ocean are the most common ways for heat energy to be redistributed. Hurricanes do not form from thunderstorms.
3. The horizontal high winds at the top of the hurricane must not come from a direction that will blow away the tops of the clouds. This is called **wind shear.** Strong wind shear high up can kill a hurricane. It's like cutting off its head and tilts the eye from a vertical to a slanted position.
4. There must first be a tropical disturbance that comes from two air masses—one hot and dry, and one warm and moist—moving over the ocean. Meteorologists are not sure quite how the disturbance becomes a hurricane. There is some force that starts it twisting, perhaps the movement of the earth below it. But this force is still unknown. They only know that this is how the hurricanes off the west coast of Africa start.

A key to harnessing a hurricane may lie in changing one of these four essential conditions.

The Anatomy of a Hurricane

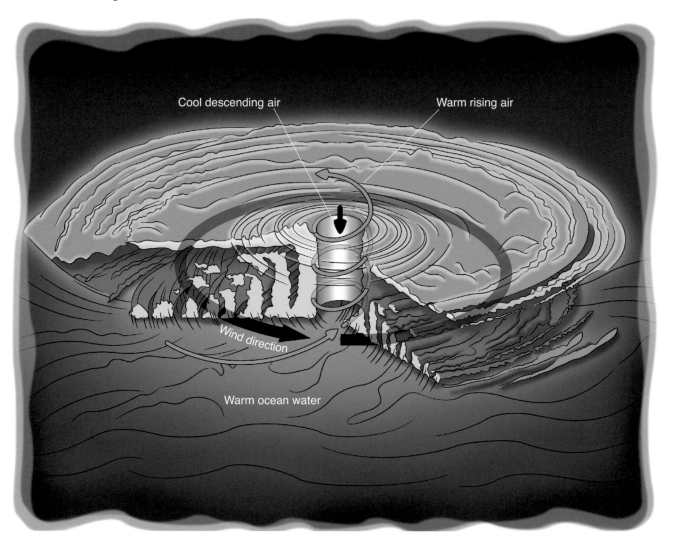

Cool descending air

Warm rising air

Wind direction

Warm ocean water

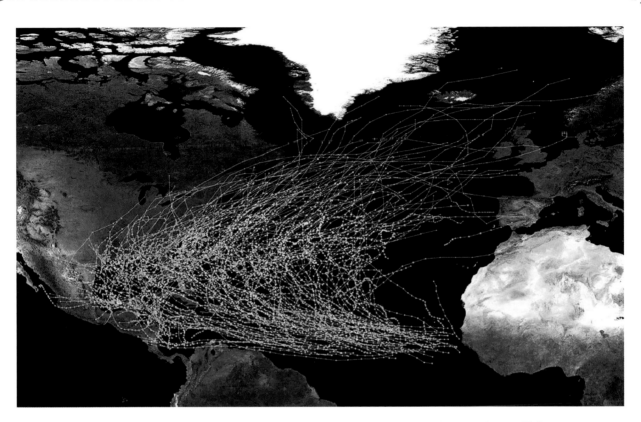

During hurricane season, from June to November, about 80 tropical disturbances form off the west coast of Africa. Only about 10 to 20 become tropical storms, which is when meteorologists give them a name. Perhaps only 10 or 11 of these develop an eye and become hurricanes, and maybe only two or three reach the United States.

The picture above shows the tracks of all tropical storms and hurricanes in the Northern Atlantic between 1980 and 2005.

TRAVELING INTO THE EYE OF THE STORM

The Life and Death of Matthew

This is a picture you don't just look at; you study it. It tells the story of Hurricane Matthew. It is a collage of a series of satellite photos, taken on different days, pasted over each other to give the storm a shape for the duration of its life. In the upper right hand corner is a numbered list of dates for Matthew, which lived from September 28, 2016 to October 10, 2016. It also tells the time of the photo—UTC means the time is coordinated with a universal time code, starting from zero, which is at the longitude of Greenwich, England. If you think of the track of the storm as almost a C, you can see the numbers corresponding to the date and time on the lower left of the storm. Each number is a different day of the storm. The colored line over the center of the storm tracks the path of the eye. On the lower left, there is a color-coded list of the categories of the storm as it traveled. So you can see by the colors on the line just how strong the storm was at different times.

In the beginning, it was a tropical storm, just missing Puerto Rico at (2). The Hurricane Hunters probably started taking measurements where

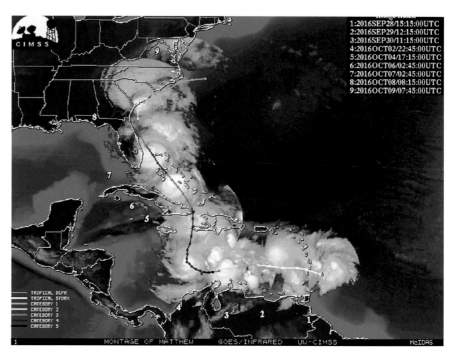

the winds were fastest since the eye had not yet formed. Then it strengthened as continued west. When it turned north (between 3 and 4) it was briefly a cat 5 over Aruba then simmered down to a Cat 4 as it passed by Haiti and Western Cuba (5). When it skirted eastern Florida (from 7 to 8) it was losing strength becoming a cat 3 and finally made landfall in South Carolina (between 8 and 9) as a Cat 1. After that the diameter of the storm widened as it weakened over land affecting a larger area. All that's left of Matthew on the last day is a lot of rain. Can you use it to tell Matthew's story in your own words?

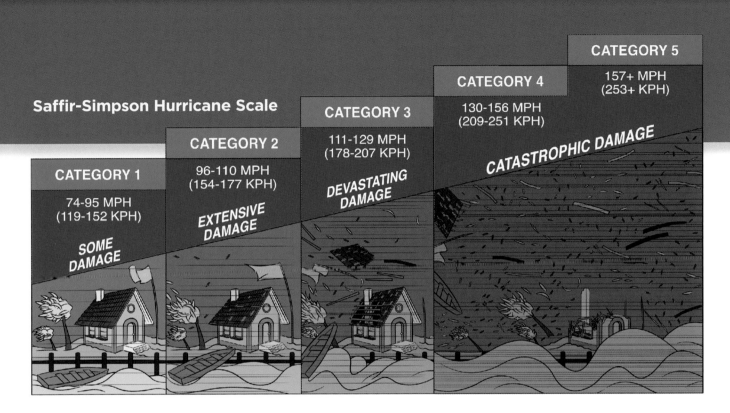

Saffir-Simpson Hurricane Scale

CATEGORY 1
74-95 MPH
(119-152 KPH)
SOME DAMAGE

CATEGORY 2
96-110 MPH
(154-177 KPH)
EXTENSIVE DAMAGE

CATEGORY 3
111-129 MPH
(178-207 KPH)
DEVASTATING DAMAGE

CATEGORY 4
130-156 MPH
(209-251 KPH)

CATEGORY 5
157+ MPH
(253+ KPH)
CATASTROPHIC DAMAGE

Meteorologists rank hurricanes according to the speed of the winds and the potential damage they can do: **Saffir-Simpson Hurricane Scale: The Simpson scale shows the destruction from winds alone. But strong winds near the coast cause destructive storm surges that result in live and property damage due to flooding.**

Weather satellites, our "eyes in the sky," have been invaluable in helping us see a hurricane grow and travel. But radar and satellite pictures are not enough. They cannot help us predict the course of the hurricane or its strength. For that, we need some very real, very accurate measurements. There is only way to get them: Fly into the center of the hurricane itself. The 53rd Weather Reconnaissance Squadron of the Air Force Reserve, also known as the Hurricane Hunters, has been doing just that since 1944. It sounds more dangerous than it has proven to be. In all this time, there has been only one crash, which occurred in 1955 and took eleven lives.

This is a picture of the eye wall of Hurricane Isabel taken from by the Hurricane Hunters. Note the plane's wing on right.

INSIDE A HURRICANE

 Q: **What is it like to fly into the eye of the storm?**

Dr. Hugh Willoughby is one of the first meteorologists to fly into a hurricane and is considered one of the world's foremost experts on these storms. He is a slightly rumpled man whose eyes light up when he talks about hurricanes. Here's how he described them to me from his bird's eye view in the storm itself:

"Hurricanes are circular storms so the wind blows around in a circle. Within the eye, but not necessarily at the center of the eye there is a calm area and wind increases outward and is strongest just at the inner edge of the wall cloud—that is, the boundary of the clear eye and the wall cloud. The wall cloud is composed of thunderstorms, convective clouds and there are strong updrafts and down drafts in the wall cloud that can make flying very bumpy.

"When you are in the wall cloud, the strongest winds are at the inner edge of it and then the wind decreases as you go outward. For an airplane flying at middle levels, say 10,000 feet, outside the wall cloud there will be bands of clouds that spiral in, and almost join the wall cloud but don't and often there will be local wind maximums in these spiral bands. And near the surface, often but not always there'll be a layer of low clouds. Above all of these is what the satellite guys call the central dense overcast (CDO) which is an area of layered clouds and the topmost clouds are just about at the lowest level of the stratosphere. If people had had satellite pictures when they decided on the names of parts of hurricanes, they would have named the eye, which can be 25 miles across, the 'belly-button.' The

eye is often clear all the way up to space. What happens is that as the updrafts rise, water gets sucked into the wall cloud and condenses forming rain and that releases the heat that the inflowing air took from the ocean (that's what makes the storm go). Outside of the eye, air is spiraling in at the surface because of the effect of friction of the wind."

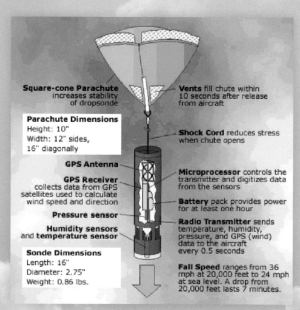

Hurricane Hunters take measurements by dropping packages of instruments called **dropsondes** that measure pressure, temperature, humidity, and wind speed in the eye wall.

Dropsondes can also be detected by the **global positioning satellites** so we can pinpoint exactly where they take the measurements. One part of every mission is to find the center of the storm at least twice and at most four times over a period of several hours. The change in position indicates which direction the storm is moving and how fast it is moving.

Changes in measurement readings indicate whether the storm is gaining or losing strength, knowledge people need so they can make preparations in case of landfall.

The Hurricane Hunters and their fleet of 10 airplanes are equipped to do recons three storms a day, twice a day during hurricane season. The information they gather is radioed back to the National Hurricane Center, where it is used to make forecasts. The data make the hurricane forecasts 30% more accurate than they would be if scientists just watched the satellite radar images. This saves a lot of lives and property. The data are also used for research so we can continue to learn about these amazing systems.

Scientists are now also studying hurricanes and the conditions that create them with the use of Hurricane Hawks—unmanned aircraft, or drones, that are controlled remotely by pilots on the ground. They can fly longer than planes without refueling, more than 28 hours, and they can fly higher than 60,000 ft (18 km). Their instruments measure the same conditions that the planes' instruments measure, from the surface to the stratosphere. Drones are yet another tool for understanding the science that underlies the formation of these deadly storms.

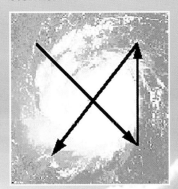

In a typical "alpha" flight path the plane makes two left turns to slice across the eye. It takes measurements called "fixes" at four points. It wIll make these four fixes several more times before heading home.

All these data gave enough information for scientists, including Dr. Hugh Willoughby, to start thinking about what could be done to weaken a hurricane. If they could lower the category by just one notch, perhaps the damage and dangers would be less severe.

PROJECT STORMFURY

Changing the weather to suit people is not a new idea. It's called **weather modification**. The most successful form is cloud seeding—making clouds form rain to end or prevent drought. Clouds are already water, but in tiny droplets that are not heavy enough to fall to earth. The thinking behind cloud seeding is to find a way to get these tiny droplets to come together to form larger, heavier drops.

Some of these droplets contain liquid water that has not frozen, although the temperature may be well below the freezing point of 32°F (0°C). This supercooled water is ready at an instant to turn into larger solid ice crystals, which melt as they fall, becoming rain. One way to make this happen is to spread the cloud with a dusting of solid crystals that can act like a core around which the supercooled water freezes. These seed crystals create a disturbance called **nucleation** that starts the crystallization process.

In 1949, an experiment by the U.S. government called Project Cirrus, 10 ounces (oz) (283 grams [g]) of solid crystals were sprayed into a cloud over New Mexico, which brought down 320 billion gallons (1,211 billion liters) of rain. In 1950, the experiment was repeated over New York, filling the city's depleted reservoirs. Scientists knew how to seed clouds, so **why not experiment and seed some hurricane clouds?** Maybe seeding the clouds just outside the eye wall could cause condensation that would release enough energy to expand the eye wall or at least, start growing another, larger eye wall causing the disintegration of the inner one. This would lower the wind speeds and take some of the punch out of the storm. There was a lot of enthusiasm from daring pilots and super-confident scientists for doing this.

Stormfury, the name of the project to modify hurricanes, was started in 1963 and lasted for about 20 years. Planes full of strapped-in scientists, piloted by daring crews, flew into hurricanes and seeded them to create an expanded eye. The problem was that the scientists were permitted to experiment only on hurricanes that had no chance of striking land or any populated area. So in the 20 years of the program, only a few hurricanes actually got seeded. In those experiments, it seemed as

> **Cloud seeding is spraying the supercooled water that's already in clouds with crystals shaped like ice crystals so that the water freezes on them, forming larger ice particles that melt as they fall, becoming rain.**

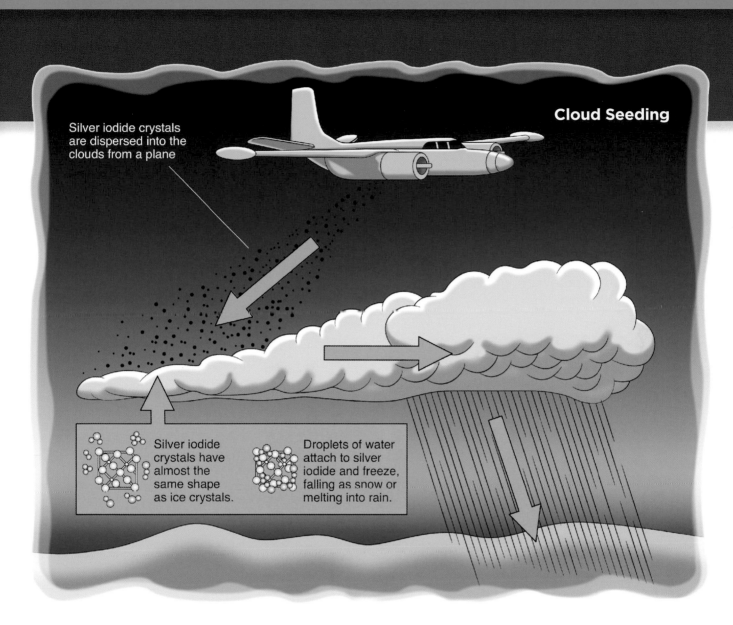

Silver iodide crystals are dispersed into the clouds from a plane

Cloud Seeding

Silver iodide crystals have almost the same shape as ice crystals.

Droplets of water attach to silver iodide and freeze, falling as snow or melting into rain.

if the eye walls expanded and wind speeds fell. But further analysis of the data just raised a lot more questions. Hugh Willoughby and a couple of other scientists concluded in the early 1980s that a second, outer eye wall can form naturally and that the weakening by cloud seeding wasn't necessarily caused by the Stormfury investigators. The second, outer eye wall is a natural part of the life cycles of the most intense hurricanes. They also found that there was

very little supercooled water in hurricanes—not enough to make seeding work.

So, although the Stormfury scientists were originally enthusiastic about the possibilities of being able to modify and weaken a hurricane, the hard, scientific results to support their hypothesis did not exist. One tough lesson for scientists is that nature never lies. And so, Project Stormfury was abandoned.

BRAINSTORMING WAYS TO HARNESS A HURRICANE

Make no mistake.
Hurricane damage is costly.

On average, hurricanes cost $1.9 billion each, but Katrina topped the charts at $125 billion and Sandy was second at $68 billion. These numbers are so large it's hard to wrap your brain around them. But the costs are high enough for people to start thinking again about investing in ways to somehow lessen the costs of picking up the pieces after one of these deadly storms.

Q: *How could we diminish the strength of a hurricane or steer it someplace where it can't destroy life or property?*

Q: **Put a Diaper on It to Absorb Water?**

Someone had the idea of dropping a patented powder called Dyn-O-Gel into the clouds that could absorb enormous quantities water, like a diaper, making the clouds disappear. In an early experiment, a small fluffy cloud disappeared after it had been treated with Dyn-O-Gel. But these kinds of clouds come and go normally. The scientists couldn't tell if the Dyn-O-Gel made the difference.

Assuming it did make a difference, here's where the math is important. When you figure out how much you'd need to knock down some of the clouds in the eye wall, it comes to almost 37,699 tons of Dyn-O-Gel. The average cargo plane can only carry 100 tons, so there would need to be 377 trips into the eye of the storm every hour and a half to keep the eye wall in a diminished state.

TRY THIS!

You can see for yourself how super-slurping plastic works by collecting it from a toddler-sized disposable diaper. Cut the edges off the diaper and remove the plastic covering. Rip the padding into small pieces and put them into a large plastic bag. Twist the bag closed and shake it for a few minutes. Collect the tiny amount of grainy powder in the bottom of the bag by shaking it into a corner and snipping it open. Place the powder in a small glass and add about 1/3 cup of water. Instantly all the water is absorbed, and no water pours out when you turn the glass over. The plastic, sodium polyacrylate, can absorb 80 times its own weight in liquid by forming a gel.

The Bomb Idea

 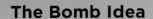

Q: *How about blowing it up with a huge bomb?*

This idea is a dead end in more than one way. Hurricanes have so much energy and are so large—hundreds of miles in diameter—that any bomb, including an atom bomb, would not give off enough energy to stop it. It's like trying to stop a moving tank by throwing rocks at it.

Since bombs give off heat, and hurricanes thrive on heat, it's possible that a bomb could make a hurricane stronger. Bombs also produce other destructive results including releasing a lot of dangerous radiation into the atmosphere, so using a bomb could be a cure worse than the disease. This has so many negatives it won't be even tried.

Mushroom Cloud of Nuclear Explosion

The afterburners on a jet spread soot into the sky.

Hurricanes are heat engines.
They transform heat from the ocean into wind. The larger the difference between the temperature at the surface of the ocean (energy input) and the temperature at the top of the eye wall (the exhaust), the stronger the hurricane. When hurricane clouds hit the cold air of the stratosphere, the water vapor condenses. This causes a tremendous release of heat energy, producing rapid expansion of air and wind that strengthens the storm.

Suppose we warm up the temperature at these high altitudes to limit condensation and the release of energy? Here are some ideas to heat up the upper atmosphere above the storm:

Q: Blacken the Clouds?
We could spray soot known as carbon black to heat up the atmosphere above a hurricane. Because black absorbs heat from the sun, this air would get warmer. This idea is losing in popularity because it will add heat to the atmosphere at a time when we're worried about the human contribution to global warming. Also, carbon black is an air pollutant.

Q: Warm Up the Top?
What if we sent jets up to the stratosphere with afterburners to heat up the air? This would lower the speed of rising air and diminish the amount of condensation from warm air that reaches the stratosphere. But it has some of the same problems of sending soot up to just blacken the clouds.

Q: Put a Shade on the Ocean?

How about preventing the ocean surface from warming up so much in the first place? Maybe by covering it with thick, bright clouds?

This is called project "Silverlining." Sea water is sprayed to create low-lying clouds that screen the ocean surface from the sun, thus keeping it cooler. Devices would spray salty seawater into the air over an area in the hurricane's path to form a layer of very dense low-lying clouds that are an especially bright white. The whiteness of the clouds would reflect a lot of the sunlight back into space, keeping the ocean below cooler. This is the device they've designed to do the job:

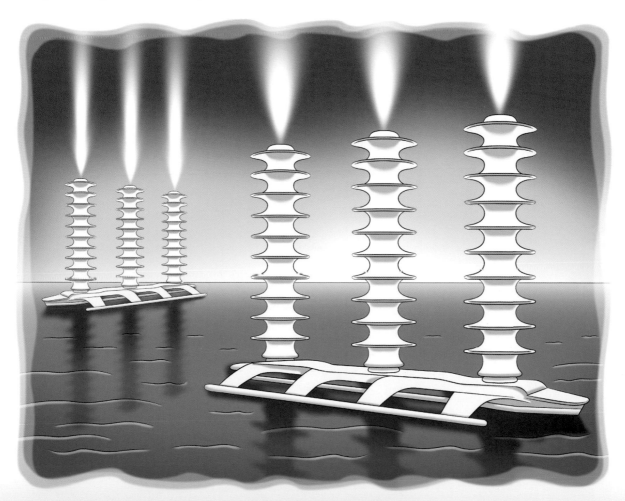

Silverlining Aerosol Spray Flotation Vehicles

Towing Ice to Cool the Path in Front of the Hurricane

Q: **Cool Down the Ocean with Ice Cubes?**
Warm ocean surface water "fuels" hurricanes. Scientists believe that if we could cool the ocean surface in the path of a hurricane by about 3°F, we could "starve" the hurricane of fuel.

Q: *How about* **hauling** *icebergs from the pole and letting them melt in the projected tropical path of a hurricane?*

This idea has a BIG math problem. How much ice would you need? How many ships would you need to tow enough ice? How much ice would melt on the journey? Would it melt fast enough to cool off the ocean? There are no real answers to these questions, but scientists guess that the numbers are big enough to make this impractical.

The average speed of a tugboat is about 10 miles per hour. So maybe, the tug could do 240 miles a day. The distance between the arctic and the Caribbean by sea is 4,358 miles. At that rate it would take 18 days, assuming it didn't run into bad weather. Would there be enough ice left to cool a substantial area of water in front of the hurricane?

 ## Put a Cover on the Ocean so Water Can't Evaporate?

How about reducing the amount of water that evaporates from the ocean surface?

One way to do this is to coat the water with a film that would prevent water molecules from escaping into the air. What kind of substance could do this? Perhaps olive oil? Or some other biodegradable chemical? Would the waves prevent this from working effectively?

 ## Throw Cold Water on the Ocean's Surface?

What about throwing cold water on the problem? Where is there a source of cold water?

Not far. One hundred meters (328 ft) below the surface, the water temperature is about 52°F (11°C). Suppose we pumped this cold water to the surface? This idea may have the best chance of succeeding because some investors, including Bill Gates, are putting money into it. The Sink Pump collects seawater as wave motion makes water splash into a basin that is above hundreds of tubes that extend down into the cold water. The pressure of the water in the sink forces surface water down to the cold area, and open valves force cold water up in another set of tubes. When it reaches the surface, the cold water spills out.

Dr. Alan Blumberg is an oceanographer especially concerned with the flow of water around coastal areas. He is interested in tides and storm surges and is involved in helping keep New York City safe from big storms like Sandy.

Dr. Alan Blumberg, an ocean scientist, with a bouncy personality, has invented another very simple pump. It takes advantage of the up and down bobbing motion of waves. The pump is a tube that extends from the surface down to the cold water below. It floats in this vertical position. When a wave comes along the tube moves up and down in place as the wave moves on. On the downward movement, the valve at the bottom opens up and water moves in. On the upward movement, the valve closes, trapping the water in the tube. With enough waves, the water is pumped from the depths to the surface bringing the cold water up. If you make the small model

> Microsoft's chairman Bill Gates is among the investors who propose using large fleets of vessels to distribute hundreds of sink pumps that would suppress hurricanes by mixing warm water from the ocean's surface with colder water at greater depths.

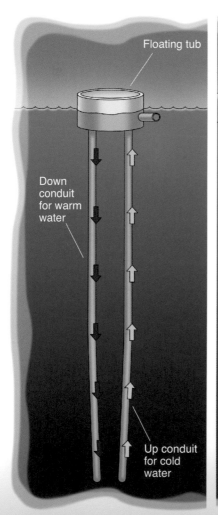

Floating tub

Down conduit for warm water

Up conduit for cold water

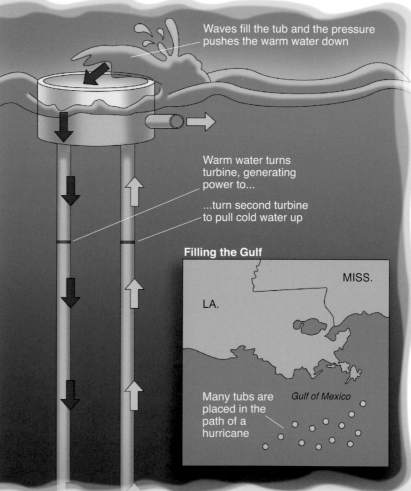

Waves fill the tub and the pressure pushes the warm water down

Warm water turns turbine, generating power to...

...turn second turbine to pull cold water up

Filling the Gulf

MISS.

LA.

Many tubs are placed in the path of a hurricane

Gulf of Mexico

The Sink Pump Uses Energy of Wave Motion

of Blumberg's pump you can bring water from below out the top. Try it. The problem with Dr. Blumberg's idea is that, although his pumps are much larger than your model, it would take 175,000 of them to cool the large area of the ocean under the hurricane's eye quickly enough to lower the temperature sufficiently to starve the hurricane. He has suggested making the tubes flexible so they can wrap around a flotation device on the top end (like a rolled sleeping bag). They would be deployed in front of the storm by squadrons of aircraft. As they fell from the sky, the tubes would unfurl by gravity and the valve end would drop down into the sea. Ta da! The pumps would be in the proper position to do their job. But what happens afterwards? How do you collect all those pumps so they don't become floating ocean debris?

Dr. Blumberg's model pump in his office is much smaller than what would be needed.

You can make a small model of Dr. Blumberg's pump. Get a small check valve and tubing to fit from an aquarium or pet store. Cut a piece of tubing about 10 in (25 cm) long and attach it to the valve, making sure that the "out" side of the valve is attached to the tube. The hard part of making this model is cutting off the plastic extension on the "in" side of the valve. When you remove the extension, you make a larger opening to take in water. You can use a large pair of scissors to snip it off. To test your pump, fill a very deep pot with water or use the bathtub, because the water needs to be deeper than the length of the tube. Put the end of the tube with the valve in the water. Prime your pump by sucking up water to the top as you would suck through a straw. Then move the pump straight up and down until you see drops of water coming out the top of the tube. Engineers often make models to test ideas.

TRY THIS!

Tube for pump should be 12 inches long

Extension on stop-check valve

Tube attaches by going around extension on valve

When the pump moves down the stop-check valve moves up as water flows in

When pump moves up the stop-check valve moves down and stops water from flowing out

Cut off with scissors

Water enters here

The tube on top attaches on this same extension

Build a Hurricane Slayer?

How about building a few monster pumps so that perhaps we only need ten?

Dr. Blumberg and an inventor partner, Rick Adler, have imagined the Blumberg-RSA Hurricane Slayer. It contains a diesel pump (like those used for sewage disposal in big cities) that pumps

Tug Towing Hurricane Slayer Into Position

Alan F. Blumberg, Stevens Institute of Technology

2 million gallons a minute! The Hurricane Slayer is HUGE—like a 30-story skyscraper. It would have to be towed into place. They figure about 10 of these across a 20-mile eye could do the job. The inventors have not released full information to the public, but they allow these pictures of their idea to be shown:

Alan F. Blumberg, Stevens Institute of Technology and colleague Rick Adler and RSA Protective Technologie

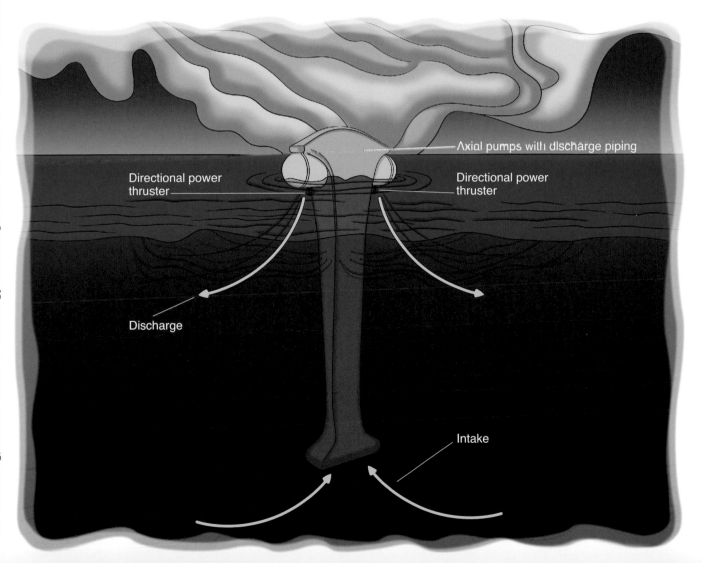

Hurricane Slayer on the Job

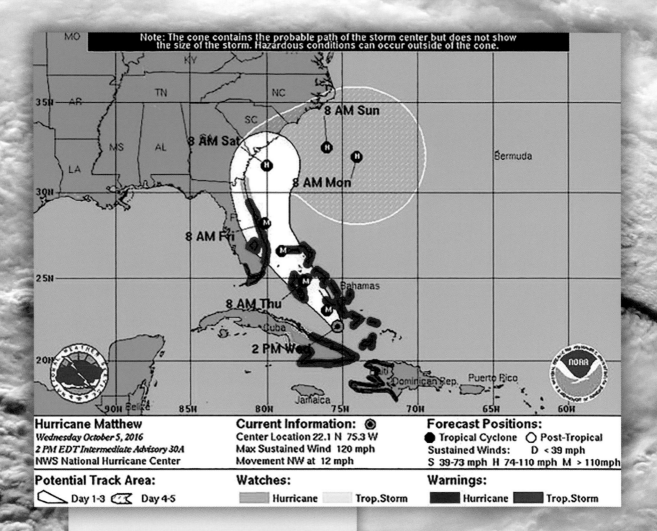

Note: The cone contains the probable path of the storm center but does not show the size of the storm. Hazardous conditions can occur outside of the cone.

Hurricane Matthew
Wednesday October 5, 2016
2 PM EDT Intermediate Advisory 30A
NWS National Hurricane Center

Current Information: ◉
Center Location 22.1 N 75.3 W
Max Sustained Wind 120 mph
Movement NW at 12 mph

Forecast Positions:
● Tropical Cyclone ○ Post-Tropical
Sustained Winds: D < 39 mph
S 39-73 mph H 74-110 mph M > 110mph

Potential Track Area:
⬭ Day 1-3 ⬭ Day 4-5

Watches:
Hurricane Trop.Storm

Warnings:
Hurricane Trop.Storm

The "cone of uncertainty" of hurricane Matthew was shown on television. The white area includes all the possibilities where the eye may pass. Meteorologists don't have enough data to predict the exact course of the storm. It suggests that it may brush the coast of North Carolina.

SHOULD WE MESS WITH MOTHER NATURE?

A hurricane is a **complicated** system.

Each measurable part—the changing temperatures, air pressures, humidity, wind speeds, directions of movement—obeys laws of physical science that are well understood. Using these laws, scientists create mathematical models on a computer. Then they plug in the specific measurements collected over time from the storm itself and let the computers crunch the numbers. This is how they calculate the path and intensity of the storm over a period of time. When the hurricane's path is shown on weather maps, it looks like a cone of possible destinations rather than narrow, direct line.

> **But the model gives people a good idea of who may be in the path of the storm, so they can make preparations.**

The farther out the projection is from the actual storm, the wider the cone. That's because there is always a range of error about exactly where the eye will make landfall.

Since all the data that describe a particular hurricane can be saved in the computer, scientists can experiment on computer-generated storms. They can, in effect, roll back the clock on a real hurricane, using all the data on it in their computer. We know what the hurricane did in real life.

What might have happened to it if they had created a small change in conditions when the hurricane was still only a tropical disturbance? Suppose they raised or lowered the temperature a few degrees, using space solar power?

In one case, they looked at Hurricane Iniki, which hit the Hawaiian island of Kauai in 1992. Their small modification, introduced about six hours before the storm was due to make landfall, was magnified over time.

As a result, they changed the course of the storm and instead of hitting the island, as the real storm did, the simulated hurricane passed west of the island.

The Computer Simulated Experiment to Change the Path of Hurricane Iniki

The white circles represent the actual path of Iniki. The black circles represent the experimeter's simulation as they ran the numbers as a control, captured by the actual hurricane. The pink circles represent the bogus path of the simulated hurricane.

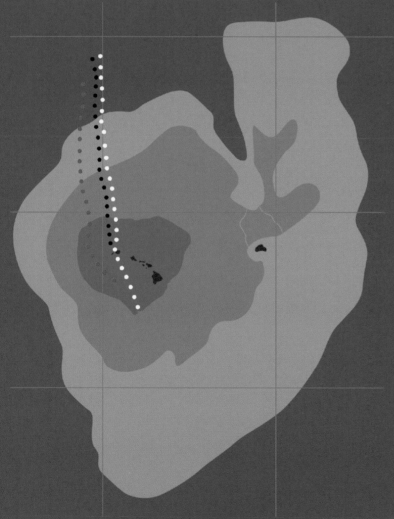

Below you see the actual path of the eye of Iniki that passed directly over the island of Kauai as a cat 4 hurricane with winds of 145 mph (233 km/h). Bullseye! Unbelievable destruction!

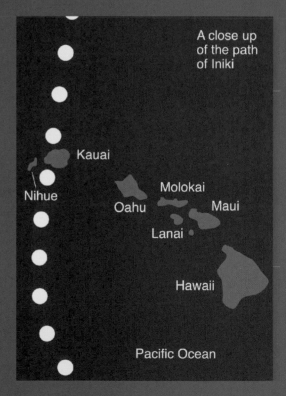

A close up of the path of Iniki

Kauai

Molokai

Nihue

Oahu

Maui

Lanai

Hawaii

Pacific Ocean

In another case, they did a simulated experiment with the brutal 1992 storm Andrew, which delivered a knockout punch to Miami, Florida, and reduced many neighborhoods to rubble. The earlier change in conditions in the experiment reduced the powerful category 3 storm to a much less damaging category 1.

A small change early in a storm that is magnified over time and can be used to affect the direction or strength of the outcome is called the **butterfly effect.** However, the mathematical models are just not good enough to accurately predict an outcome.

We would have to run a lot of models to figure out just what the butterfly effect should be to change the storm and when and where it needs to be delivered to produce a good outcome, or even several different outcomes. This means running many mathematical models with accurate starting information over a period of time. No matter how powerful the computer, this takes time, and a good answer might not be discovered in time to make it happen. There is also a very real chance of making a mistake that backfires. Suppose we made a small change on a hurricane headed for New Orleans and it made a left turn and slammed into Cuba? One BIG international headache!

> On the other hand, hurricanes serve the earth in many positive ways.

They are heat valves, letting heat that builds up in the ocean escape to the upper atmosphere. They bring rain to parts of the world that would be too dry for the people who live there to survive

without them. Maybe it's our own fault that hurricanes create so much destruction. Does it make sense to build expensive, high-rise, luxury buildings on vulnerable coastlines? Development has destroyed much natural vegetation along coastlines that acted as a buffer against storm surges. When hurricanes pass over land, they quickly lose strength. Coastal wetlands that sapped hurricanes of power have been destroyed. So there is little natural protection left.

Climate change will have some influence on the frequency and size of these destructive storms. Although we don't yet know what will happen specifically, scientists say to look for "weird weather events." There is no doubt that human activity influences climate and weather. We must be careful about what we do.

> One thing is certain: Human activities produce unintended consequences.

We must not forget that our planet is precious. So before we actually try to harness a hurricane we need to know a great deal more. Maybe you are now fascinated enough to get in the game.

GLOSSARY OF TERMS
as They Apply to Hurricanes

afterburner—a jet aircraft device that increases the thrust of a supersonic plane. It burns an extra amount of fuel, which is left behind as a trail of black smoke.

air pressure—the weight of a column of air 1 square inch (or 1 square centimeter) that goes up to the end of the atmosphere.

atmosphere—a sea of air covering the earth. It is made up of layers. We live at the bottom of the bottom layer, the troposphere. All of the layers together, including the top layer—the ionosphere—are about 526 miles (847 km) thick.

barometer—an instrument to measure air pressure and predict changes in the weather.

butterfly effect—a small change in initial weather conditions as a storm is forming that has a large effect on the power or direction of the storm later on.

carbon black—finely distributed carbon particles (soot) that can blacken the sky behind jet afterburners.

climate change—a long-term change in average weather of a region of the earth due to global warming. Scientists have evidence that there is an increased amount of carbon dioxide in the atmosphere due to the burning of fossil fuels. This has a greenhouse effect on the atmosphere, preventing heat from escaping.

clockwise—circular movement in the same direction as the hands of a clock—a turn to the right.

clouds—condensation of water vapor in the air into droplets. Fair-weather clouds are white. Storm clouds block the sun and appear gray or dark gray.

condensation—the change of state of water vapor, which is a gas, into liquid water. Heat is released during this process.

convection current—the wind that is created as cooler dense air rushes in to take the place of rising warmer air.

Coriolis effect—apparent change in the path of an object that is part of a rotating system. The earth, for example, rotates fastest at the equator, because it turns the longest distance in 24 hours. Latitudes north and south of the equator move more slowly. This difference in speed appears to give a counterclockwise twist to storms in the northern hemisphere and a clockwise twist to storms in the southern hemisphere.

counterclockwise—circular movement that is opposite to the direction of the hands of a clock—a turn to the left.

dropsonde—a disposable package of weather-measuring instruments with a parachute designed to be dropped by an airplane that is flying into a storm. Many dropsondes are used in many missions over time to discover the power and track of a hurricane or typhoon.

energy—a measurable property of matter that can be transferred to other matter. It can take many forms—motion, electricity, heat, light, chemical, nuclear energy—but the total amount of energy in any system is conserved. We can account for where it came from and where it goes.

evaporation—the change in state from a liquid to a gas. Energy is needed to make water change into water vapor.

eye wall—the swirling clouds that form the eye of a hurricane. They contain the strongest updrafts and downdrafts, generating the winds spiraling out from the eye.

global positioning satellites—a system of satellites, computers, and receivers that allows us to calculate the latitude and longitude of any position on the planet.

heat engine—a system that uses heat to generate motion. A hurricane can be thought of as a heat engine that moves heat from the surface of the ocean to the stratosphere.

hot tower—a very tall cloud that reaches the top of the troposphere and is associated with powerful tropical storms. The cold air temperature causes rapid condensation in the hot tower, releasing enormous amounts of heat resulting in expansion of air and violent updrafts from the sea.

humidity—the amount of water vapor in the air. High humidity in the summer reduces the amount of sweat that can evaporate and cool the skin. So humid days feel warmer than dryer days.

hurricane—an intense counterclockwise circular storm that forms in the northern hemisphere with a clearly defined eye at the center and wind speeds of at least 74 mph (119 km/h).

hurricane eye—the center of a hurricane, surrounded by the eye wall of clouds. It can be cloudless all the way up to the stratosphere and has the lowest air pressure of the storm.

Hurricane Hawks—drones (remote controlled flying devices that can take the same measurements as dropsondes by flying into hurricanes)

Hurricane Hunters—a team of pilots and meteorologists who do research on violent storms by flying into them and taking measurements of temperature, air pressure, and humidity. The data are put into computers to calculate and predict the strength of the storms and their path.

hurricane season—June 1 to November 30. Peak activity is from mid-August to mid-October.

Iniki—the category 4 hurricane that struck the island of Kauai in Hawaii in September of 1992. Using the data from Iniki, scientists changed the temperature of the storm on a computer early in its development, which made the path of the storm go west of the island. This was a simulated experiment demonstrating the butterfly effect.

Katrina—a category 5 hurricane over the Gulf Coast that weakened to a category 3 when it struck the Louisiana shore in late August of 2005. With a total property damage of $108 billion, it was the costliest natural disaster in US history.

landfall—when a storm moves over land. Landfall for a hurricane is when the eye of the storm reaches land.

mercury—a liquid metal 13 times heavier than water first used to measure air pressure in a barometer.

meteorologists—scientists who study weather.

molecules—the smallest particles of matter made up of two or more atoms.

nitrogen—a colorless, odorless, gaseous element that makes up 78% of air. Nitrogen atoms hook together to form two-atom molecules.

oxygen—a colorless, odorless, gaseous element that makes up about 20% of the earth's atmosphere. Like nitrogen, oxygen in the air is made up of two-atom molecules.

precipitation—condensation of water in the atmosphere that is heavy enough to fall to earth as rain, snow, sleet, or hailstones.

Saffir-Simpson Hurricane Wind Scale—a system of classifying hurricanes based on sustained wind speed. The first category is 74 mph (119 km/h). Category 5 is the strongest with wind speeds of 156 mph (250 km/h) and higher.

sink pump—a pump that collects water into a basin at the water's surface through tubes that descend into the water. Wave motion opens and closes valves to force the water up the tubes into the basin.

storm surge—water that winds have pushed ahead of the hurricane creating a huge wave (almost 33 feet [10 m] high)

stratosphere—the layer of the earth's atmosphere above the troposphere. It starts about 6–11 miles (almost 10–18 km) above the earth's surface and extends about 31 miles (50 km). Jet airplanes travel in the lower levels of the stratosphere because there is no weather here.

temperature—the amount of hotness or coldness of a substance. It is measured with thermometers.

TRMM—NASA's Tropical Rainfall Measuring Mission monitors and studies tropical rainfall using a special weather satellite. The probe was deactivated on April 9, 2015, after taking some amazing pictures of cloud structures in hurricanes, particularly pictures of hot towers.

tropical disturbance—a low-pressure mass of air that may develop into a tropical storm.

tropical storm—a low-pressure mass of air that organizes into a rotating system.

troposphere—The layer of the atmosphere closest to the earth where weather occurs. It is about 6–11 miles (almost 10–18 km) thick.

vacuum—the absence of any matter, including air.

vertical wind shear—a sudden increase in horizontal winds that can cut off the top of a hurricane, making it less powerful. It can tilt the vertical direction of rising convection currents in a storm.

weather—the local conditions of temperature, air pressure, humidity, and precipitation.

weather modification—the attempt by scientists to change local weather conditions for human benefit.

weather satellite—a device that is put in orbit to photograph and measure weather conditions and send these measurements to meteorologists' computers. A system of weather satellites is used to predict weather with a great deal more accuracy than in the past.

SELECTED BIBLIOGRAPHY

Carson, Mary Kay. *Inside Hurricanes.* New York: Sterling, 2010.

Cullen, Heidi. *The Weather of the Future: Heat Waves, Extreme Storms, and Other Scenes from a* Davies, Pete. *Inside the Hurricane: Face to Face with Nature's Deadliest Storms.* New York: Henry Holt, 2000.

Demerest, Chris L. *Hurricane Hunters! Riders on the Storm.* New York: Margaret K. McElderry Books, 2006.

Emanuel, Kerry. *Divine Wind: The History and Science of Hurricanes.* New York: Oxford University Press, 2005.

Fradin, Judy, and Dennis Fradin. *Hurricanes: Witness to Disaster.* Washington, D.C.: National Geographic, 2007.

Gibbons, Gail. *Hurricanes.* New York: Holiday House, 2009.

Hoffman, Ross N. "Controlling Hurricanes: Can Hurricanes and Other Severe Tropical Storms Be Moderated or Deflected?" *Scientific American*, October 1, 2004.

Lauber, Patricia. *Hurricanes: Earth's Mightiest Storms.* New York: Scholastic Press, 1996.

Leatherman, Stephen P., Jack Williams. *Hurricanes: Causes, Effects, and the Future.* Minneapolis, Minn.: Voyageur Press, 2008.

Mooney, Chris. *Storm World: Hurricanes, Politics, and the Battle Over Global Warming.* New York: Harcourt, 2007.

Silverstein, Alvin, Virginia Silverstein, and Laura Silverstein Nunn. *Hurricanes: The Science Behind Killer Storms.* Berkeley Heights, N.J.: Enslow, 2010.

Simon, Seymour. *Hurricanes.* New York: HarperCollins, 2007.

Treaster, Joseph B. *Hurricane Force: In the Path of America's Deadliest Storms.* Boston: Kingfisher, 2007.

Links

Hurricane Hunters:
www.hurricanehunters.com

To do a "cyber flight into the eye of a hurricane":

www.hurricanehunters.com/
cyberflight.htm

National Hurricane Center:
www.nhc.noaa.gov

Saffir-Simpson Hurricane Wind Scale: www.nhc.noaa.gov/aboutsshws.php. This has an animation of damage done to a house as the wind speed increases to category 5.

United States Geological Survey—Science for a Changing World: www.usgs.gov/science/science-explorer?lq=hurricane+season+is+here

Two videos Vicki Cobb made while doing her research for the book:

Meet the Meteorologists—
vimeo.com/65865182

The Hurricane Slayer—
vimeo.com/66414718

AUTHOR'S NOTE

A hurricane is the largest storm on the planet with the power to destroy life and property. It is also a fascinating system and the focus of intense scientific study. In my research I traveled to Florida, home of the National Hurricane Center and Boston, home of the Massachusetts Institute of Technology, and Hoboken, NJ to the Stevens Institute of Technology. I wish to thank the following people for their contribution to my education about hurricanes. Dr. Stephen "Dr. Beach" P. Leatherman and his wife Debbie for their hospitality and insights; Dr: Hugh Willoughby for stories of the history of the Hurricane Hunters and Project Stormfury. Dr. Kerry Emmanual of MIT for his passion and curiosity about the origin of hurricanes and saving the planet; Dr. Alan Blumberg, Director of the Davidson Laboratory, Stevens Institute of Technology, and his colleague Rick Adler, of RSA Protective Technologies, for sharing their creative inventions for cooling the surface of the ocean that might actually be feasible some day; and for Dr. Chris Landsea, Martin C. Nelson, Keqi Zhang for showing me around the National Hurricane Center. In addition I would also like to thank Roberta Fisher, for her personal story of surviving Andrew, Ken Caldeira, Department of Global Ecology, Carnegie Institution for Science, Dennis Feltgen and Erica Rule of NOAA for helping facilitate my research.

Special thanks Dr. Stephen Leatherman for review of the manuscript but I accept full responsibility for the accuracy of its content.

A big shout-out to my editor Barbara Ciletti for her enduring patience through many sets of complicated proofs and for keeping the narrative moving along.

All photos have been graciously supplied from NASA and NOAA unless indicated otherwise. The collage photo on page 22 has been amplified through the technology of The Cooperative Institute for Meteorologic Satellite Studies.

INDEX

Illustrations are indicated by **boldface.** When illustrations fall within a page span, the entire span of pages is **boldface.**

To Susan Schulman, who has been my friend, agent, and partner in many endeavors through a couple of decades of all kinds of weather.

Quarto is the authority on a wide range of topics.
Quarto educates, entertains, and enriches the lives of our readers—
enthusiasts and lovers of hands-on living.
www.quartoknows.com

© 2017 Quarto Publishing Group USA Inc.
Published by Seagrass Press,
an imprint of The Quarto Group
All rights reserved. Seagrass is a registered trademark.

Text © 2017 Vicki Cobb
Illustrations by Theo Cobb
Photos on page 15 by Vicki Cobb; page 25 (Dr. Hugh Willoughby) compliments of Florida International University; page 35 by Dr. Alan Blumberg;
page 53 (Dr. Alan Blumberg) compliments of Stevens Institute. Photos on pages 1, 4, 29, 41, and 42–47 Shutterstock. All other photos are by NASA or NOAA.

All rights reserved. No part of this book may be reproduced in any form without written permission of the copyright owners. All images in this book
have been reproduced with the knowledge and prior consent of the artists concerned, and no responsibility is accepted by producer, publisher,
or printer for any infringement of copyright or otherwise, arising from the contents of this publication. Every effort has been made to ensure that
credits accurately comply with information supplied. We apologize for any inaccuracies that may have occurred and will resolve inaccurate or
missing information in a subsequent reprinting of the book.

6 Orchard Road, Suite 100
Lake Forest, CA 92630
quartoknows.com
Visit our blogs at quartoknows.com

Reproduction of work for study or finished art is permissible. Any art produced or photomechanically reproduced from this
publication for commercial purposes is forbidden without written consent from the publisher, Seagrass Press.

Printed in China
1 3 5 7 9 10 8 6 4 2

MIX
Paper from
responsible sources
FSC® C101537